To Melody and Johnny
—T.R.

The editors would like to thank
BARBARA KIEFER, PhD,
Charlotte S. Huck Professor of Children's Literature,
The Ohio State University,
DEBRA COLODNER, PhD, Director of Education,
MARK DIMMITT, PhD, Director of Natural History, and
MARIE LONG, Interpretive Programs Manager,
Arizona-Sonora Desert Museum,
for their assistance in the preparation of this book.

Visit us on the Web!
Seussville.com
rhcbooks.com

Educators and librarians, for a variety of teaching tools, visit us at RHTeachersLibrarians.com

Library of Congress Cataloging-in-Publication Data is available upon request.
ISBN 978-0-375-85868-0 (trade) — ISBN 978-0-593-81417-8 (lib. bdg.)
ISBN 978-0-593-12679-0 (ebook)

MANUFACTURED IN CHINA
36 35 34 33 32 31 30 29 28 27
2024 Random House Children's Books Edition

Why Oh Why Are Deserts Dry?

All About
DESERTS

by Tish Rabe

illustrated by Aristides Ruiz and Joe Mathieu

The Cat in the Hat's Learning Library®

Random House 🏠 New York

I'm the Cat in the Hat,
and today is the day
that we're off to see deserts.
Let's leave right away!

You may think that deserts
are empty and bare,
but you'll be surprised by
the things we'll find there—

insects and lizards,
flowers and snow.
Want to see for yourself?
Buckle up and let's go!

Why are deserts dry?
I'll be glad to explain.
There are very few clouds
above them to bring rain.

Without clouds, there is nothing
to block the sun's light
or to hold the heat in,
so it gets cold at night.

The air is so dry
any rain deserts get
dries up right away,
so they do not stay wet.

Without water, surviving
in deserts is rough.
Plants, insects, and animals
need to be tough.

All living things need
to have water, so how
do they live where it's dry?
I will show you right now.

Desert plants must find water.
Some have ways to store it.
Roots spread out to find it
or reach deep down for it.

Shallow roots of this cactus
pull water through them.
The cactus then stores it
inside of its stem.

There's a tree in the desert
that's called a mesquite.
Its roots reach for water
that's down forty feet!

The Sonoran Desert
is where we will find
a very big cactus
that's one of a kind!

It's called the saguaro,
and I have been told
it can grow to be over
two hundred years old.

"suh-**WAR**-oh"

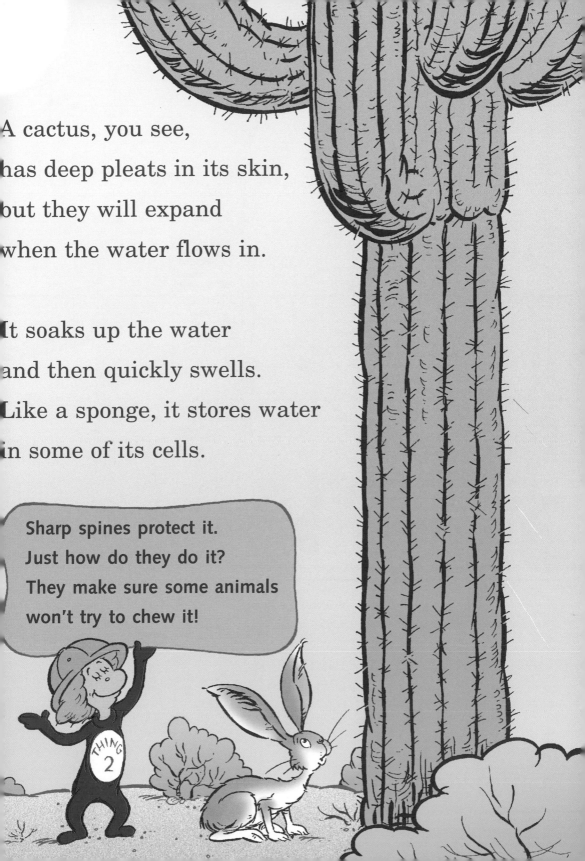

A cactus, you see,
has deep pleats in its skin,
but they will expand
when the water flows in.

It soaks up the water
and then quickly swells.
Like a sponge, it stores water
in some of its cells.

Sharp spines protect it.
Just how do they do it?
They make sure some animals
won't try to chew it!

This Gila woodpecker
knows very well
that a cactus will serve
as the perfect hotel.

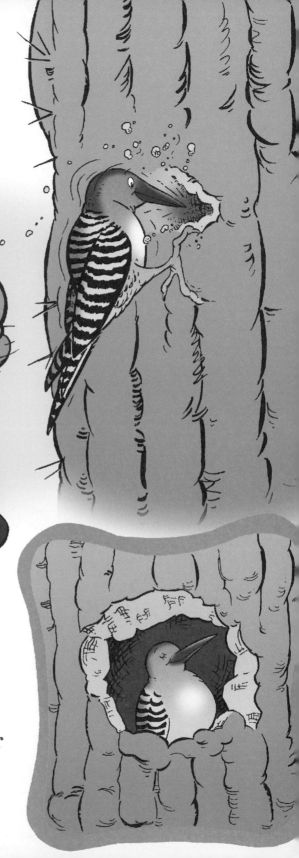

"HEE-luh"

She pecks a small hole
and then slips inside.
It's cool and it gives her
a safe place to hide.

When she's ready to leave,
well, I have little doubt
someone else will move in
after she has moved out!

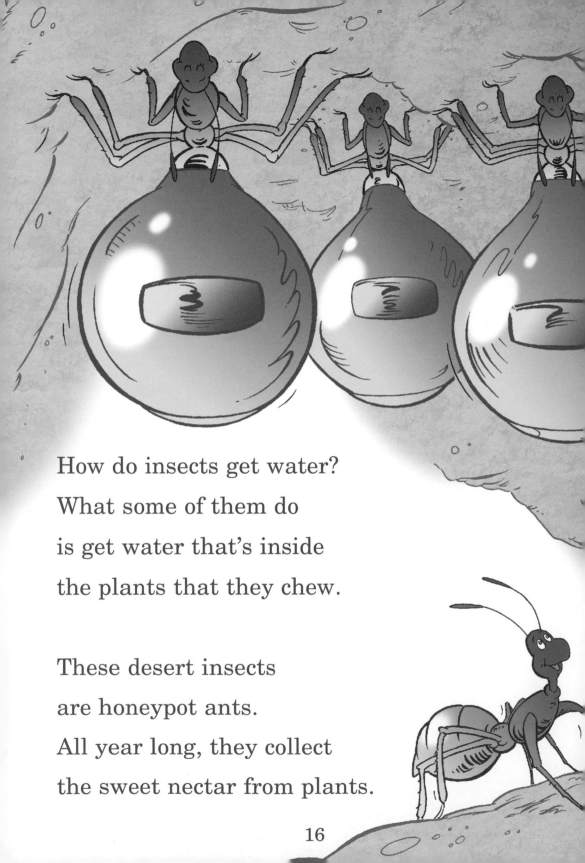

How do insects get water?
What some of them do
is get water that's inside
the plants that they chew.

These desert insects
are honeypot ants.
All year long, they collect
the sweet nectar from plants.

They store it inside them,
and then they can feed it
to ants who are hungry
whenever they need it!

The Namib Desert
gets rain rarely, and yet
fog comes from the sea
and makes everything wet.

Here the fog-basking beetle
has a way to survive,
getting water it needs
to help it stay alive.

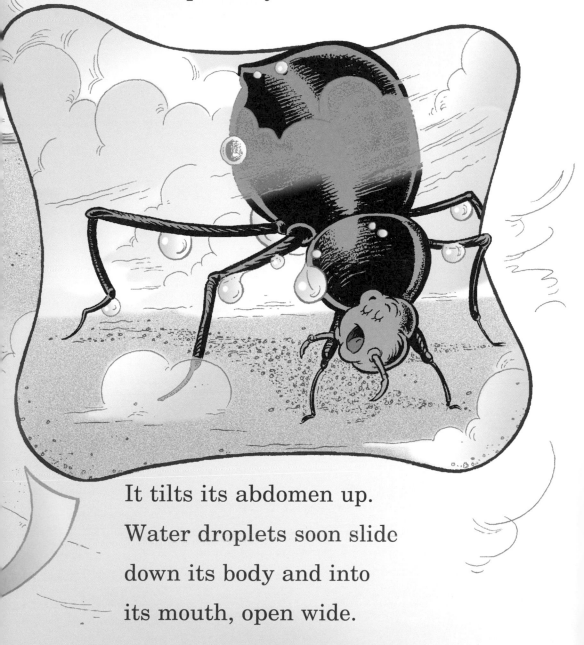

It tilts its abdomen up.
Water droplets soon slide
down its body and into
its mouth, open wide.

Animals differ
in the food that they eat
and the ways they keep cool
in the dry desert heat.

In the daytime, small animals
stay underground.
Later on, when it's cooler,
they move aboveground.

This cute fennec fox's
furry-soled feet
help him walk on hot sand.
His big ears let out heat.

Kangaroos lick their arms
to help cool off their skin,
then each digs a hole
in the ground and climbs in.

We asked this lizard
how he spends his days.
Each morning, he's warmed
by the sun's gentle rays.

By midday, it's hotter
and it's time to hide.
He slips into his burrow
and goes deep inside.

In the late afternoon,
he is back in the sun.
It is not as hot now,
and the day's almost done.

Then he's back in his burrow
to sleep through the night.
He'll be up with the sun
just as soon as it's light.

Hawks, eagles, and vultures
fly high in the air.

They stay off the ground.
It's much cooler up there.

Kangaroo rat never drinks,
but she eats lots of seeds.
The water inside them
is all that she needs.

Roadrunners can fly,
but they usually run.
They catch lizards and snakes
in the hot desert sun.

The Sahara Desert,
geographers say,
is almost as big
as the whole U.S.A.

Here the crowned sandgrouse
flies high in the sky,
miles and miles to find water,
and I'll tell you why.

His babies are thirsty
and waiting for him,
so when he finds water
he quickly flies in.

He soaks his feathers
until they are wet.
This water is all that
his babies will get.

They drink from his feathers,
which dry soon, and then
he must take to the sky
to find water again.

Out here in the desert,
when winds start to blow,
there are few plants to help
hold the sand down, and so . . .

the wind blows the sand,
which forms into dunes.
It makes shapes in the sand
like these crescent moons.

What's this nomad wearing?

It's called a burnoose.

It protects him from sun.

It is long and it's loose.

People called nomads
spend their whole lives here.
They move place to place
and keep moving all year.

In the Mojave Desert,
plants bloom, grow, and die,
but they leave seeds behind
in the ground, and that's why

when it rains, these seeds burst
into flowers so bright
there's a rainbow of colors—
a beautiful sight.

"mo-HA-vee"

They will not live long,
but before it is over
there are lilies, primroses,
sunflowers, owl clover.

Some flowers stay open
for only one day.
Hummingbirds drink their nectar
and then fly away.

In the shimmering heat
of the sun's burning glare,

you might think you see something
that's not really there.

This is called a mirage.
It's a bit like a dream.
Things you think you are seeing
are not what they seem.

mih-RAHJ

When you get a bit closer,
things fade out of sight.
They were not there at all.
It's a trick of the light.

In a dry, dusty desert,
if you suddenly see
something green up ahead
like some plants or a tree,

"oh-**AY**-sis"

this is called an oasis.
Where these plants are growing,
somewhere in the ground
there is water that's flowing.

Some deserts are hot
in the sun's burning light,
but the temperature falls
and it gets cold at night.

Then the world comes alive
with owls, foxes, and bats,
coyote and rabbits,
mice, deer, and rats.

34

Nocturnal animals
come out, and soon
they search to find food
by the light of the moon.

Before the sun rises,
they all disappear.
You would think all the animals
never were here!

Not all deserts are hot!
The next place we'll go
is the Gobi, and here
we will find ice and snow.

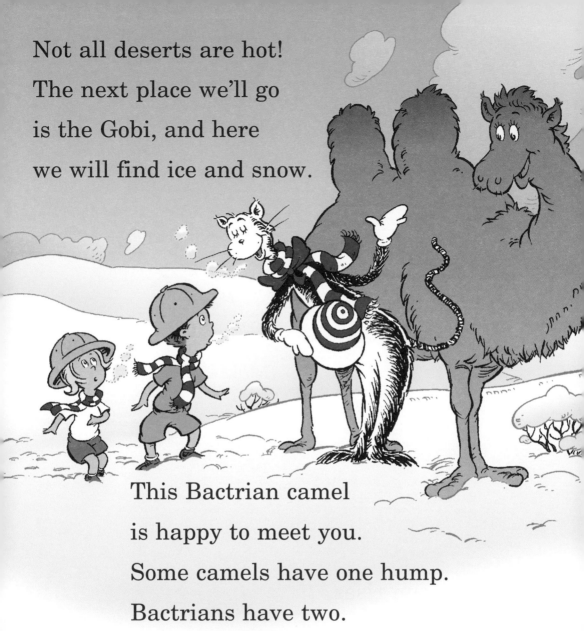

This Bactrian camel
is happy to meet you.
Some camels have one hump.
Bactrians have two.

If he goes a long time
without eating or drinking,
the humps on his back
start steadily shrinking.

They're not filled with water
but instead contain fat.
When he can't eat or drink,
he keeps going on that.

I filled up my bathtub
and filled up my sink.
That's about at one time
what a camel can drink.

He can drink thirty gallons
of water, and then
he can go a whole week
before he drinks again!

Antarctica is the largest
desert of all.
The air is so cold here
that rain does not fall.

This desert is covered
with ice and with snow.
The ice never melts here
and freezing winds blow.

It is dark in the winter
and cold through the year.
Though scientists visit,
no people live here!

Penguins have a way
to survive the cold weather.
They get close to each other
and huddle together.

Today you've seen things
that few people will see,
and I am so happy
you saw them with me.

A desert, it's true,
is a harsh habitat,
but I hope you've discovered
it's much more than that.

No day in a desert
is ever the same,
and once you've been there
you are glad

that you came.

GLOSSARY

Abdomen: The largest of the three sections of an adult insect's body.

Burnoose: A loose-fitting robe worn by people in the desert.

Burrow: A hole dug in the ground by an animal.

Cell: A small unit of living matter.

Differ: To be unlike, or different.

Geologist: A scientist who studies the structure and physical changes of the earth.

Glare: A strong, unpleasant light.

Habitat: The place where a plant or animal lives.

Mirage: A false image of an object that is seen at a distance but isn't really there.

Nocturnal: Appearing at night.

Oasis: A place in a desert where shrubs, trees, and other plants can grow because there is a supply of water.

Shimmering: Shining with a faint, flickering light.

LEARN MORE WITH THESE FUN ACTIVITIES

Make a desert packing list!

Imagine what you'd bring on a trip to the desert with this memory game! Start the game by saying, "I'm going to the desert, and I'm bringing . . ." Then name something you'll need. You might pick sunscreen for protection or a jacket for the cold nights. The next person says the same thing, listing your item and adding an item of their own. As the game goes on, each person adds to the list! You're out of the game when you can't remember the list anymore. The last person remaining wins!

Plant a cactus!

A cactus doesn't need a lot of water to survive, making it the perfect desert plant! You can grow a cactus at home in a small pot and special soil. Be sure to keep it somewhere it can get plenty of sunlight, and water it when the soil is dry.

Paint with sand!

Many deserts have lots of sand. On a piece of construction paper, use glue to draw the outline of something you might see in a desert, like a lizard or tortoise. An adult can help you sprinkle sand over the paper while the glue is still wet. When the glue dries, the sand will stick to the paper to reveal your drawing!

INDEX